LoveSpeaks

...because love has its OWN language

Marvette Camille

Order this book online at www.trafford.com
or email orders@trafford.com

Most Trafford titles are also available at major online book retailers.

Printed in the United States of America.

ISBN: 978-1-4907-4285-4 (sc)
     978-1-4907-4284-7 (e)

Because of the dynamic nature of the Internet, any web addresses or links contained in this book may have changed since publication and may no longer be valid. The views expressed in this work are solely those of the author and do not necessarily reflect the views of the publisher, and the publisher hereby disclaims any responsibility for them.

Our mission is to efficiently provide the world's finest, most comprehensive book publishing service, enabling every author to experience success. To find out how to publish your book, your way, and have it available worldwide, visit us online at www.trafford.com

Any people depicted in stock imagery provided by Thinkstock are models,
and such images are being used for illustrative purposes only.
Certain stock imagery © Thinkstock.

Trafford rev. 10/15/2014

North America & international
toll-free: 1 888 232 4444 (USA & Canada)
fax: 812 355 4082

Table of Contents

Acknowledgements

There will never be a time wherein my first acknowledgement in any book I write, will not go to the Almighty for choosing to gift me with the ability to string my words together a little differently than others, so as to be able to call myself a writer. I have never and will never take any praise for this ability, but will, in showing my sincerest gratitude, always use the gift I was given, and try my best to use it for the greater good. Next, I would like to say a humongous thank you to Kemmone Hall, my editor; a very good writer in her own right, who had to put up with so many emails from me in the course of editing LoveSpeaks, that I lost count a long time ago.

Thank you is nowhere near enough for Mike Christie, the person who created the cover of the book in one go, after simply asking me what I had in mind. Hey, "the other MC" you ROCK iyah!! A world of thanks also goes out to my friend Vanessa Ellis for creating the hearts that the pieces are typed in. She did a number of different ones before deciding on which one to use. Thank you so much girl, hope you have forgiven me for being so pestiferous throughout the process. Thanks also go out to those persons who are always encouraging me to keep writing, and not just to write, but also to publish the material that I write.

Like I always say, writing is one thing, but having the courage to send what I refer to as "my babies" out there for all to see and (yikes), yes to criticize, is an extremely vulnerable place to be. As such, I truly appreciate all the constant encouragement I have been receiving from family members and friends. As I continue to write; since writing for me is a need rather than a want, I crave your continued support and am confident I will receive it for all my future writing projects. Thanks all!!

1

Love's Melody

He plays me like an out-of-control fiddle, with the melodies haunting and piercing the deepest recesses of my wayward soul. He strums my "buttons" that are otherwise hidden from plain view, but that which are so exposed to him so that he can pluck at them so soulfully even with eyes closed and hands tied behind his back.

He beats that special sound on my heart that resonates within an alcove of tunes that have the same effect as whip cream on strawberries. He re-arranges the levels of my chords as he picks at the strings of my fully-surrendered heart, as I exhale in falsetto having lost the ability to be my own master.

We compose a duet that swells to a MIGHTY crescendo that alters the timing of our breathing, as we are taken to a space of expressionism wherein we can scarce contain the musical feelings within. There are no flat areas in this musical interlude that is filled with a mixture of harmony, which modulates to keys higher than we thought we could reach.

There is no room for monotones, as the repertoire of his love-musicology is too vast to be subjected to repetitions. He creates nocturnes that are meant only for me; that push me to octaves beyond my natural realm. I become an opera, an entire orchestra, where my pitch is extended to its contralto level and I am unable to operate my vocals normally.

I break into a recital of my deepest feelings as I try to match the rhythm of my own heart beat. He serenades me as I slip into a symphony that is an expression of what is reverberating through my entire being. The timbre of his harmonious strumming has now become the instrument of the power he holds over me, while I struggle against being completely saturated by his powerful melodies.

The tonality of his ability to "play me" is Instrumental in visibly affecting the way I breathe, and I fight to stay on key as I lose control of my voice with vocal cords that have now become out of tune with the erratic beating of my heart, but instead are absolutely in-tuned to him.

Strum me, play me, serenade the hell out of me, elevate me to a soprano as I relish in the feelings of the loss of control, when I surrender to the SWEETNESS of you!!.

Open-Heart "Lovery"

Bleeding love, bleeding you, from a place that goes "thumpity thump" in a surgery performed on love-sick parts that are too weak not to surrender to you.

My ticker is in atrophy and it is all about the cardiac; fibrosis sets in and my heart is stretched thin and forceps grasp my expanding heart muscles as it sticks me like a pin.

No, it's not gastric & it will take more than just plastic, to restart a heart, now falling apart, when love is not reciprocated.

Hurry up, STAT; help me, show me how
- to restore a heart that is ready to
depart, from things platonic,
to things romantic, to
frolic in future
enchantment.

Love's Compulsion

I love because the choice was taken away from me by a heart that listens to what it was created to do. The depth of my feelings springs forth and I am compelled to feel; even against my own rebellious will to hide all I feel inside.

I need to love, but also want to love, as even if the need was taken away, I would still be left with a want that surpasses any resistance my mind would think to put up. Love often times asks why, but then the answer is embedded so deep within me that the why becomes negated and replaced with "I have to."

Feelings with no explanations, saturate my being and leaving me helpless against something as old as time, sweeter than candy; something divinely planned & more precious than any agenda we have to manipulate our feelings and re-direct our thoughts.

Drawn in by something that is bigger than us, stronger than us - that pulls us in and keeps us there against our will, even when we want to run to the hills. It's a need that consumes us, a want that pervades us, a truth that we can't hide from, even when we tell ourselves otherwise.

Love chases us and when we are caught, it captures our attention and keeps us riveted to a spell-binding performance that takes our breath away.

In Love With Love

Eyes closed, shutting out everything but you

Lips licked and primed, impatiently awaiting your warmth against mine,

Trembling from its intensity—I surrender to your allure

Captured in the essence of you, basking in the presence of you,

moved by the tapestry of all that draws me to you without my consent.

Outnumbered & out-matched by something too powerful to resist,

I travel out of body, moved to a place where nothing but love resides;

A place where all is love & love is everything!

Love's Pervasion

A well-spring of all that propels life & gives it meaning—all wrapped up in a word so small, yet one that encapsulates all that we are. A universe-filled vastness that overshadows any beauty your eyes could ever behold.

Nothing compares and life is nothing without it. We can pretend we don't want it, even say we can live without it, but when all is said and done, even if we try to ignore it; it is everywhere, even where we aren't looking for it.

Love has never done wrong, is too pure to be mistaken for anything else, too kind to hurt....and in its truest form it never fails. It is everywhere, you can't escape it, but why would you want to when it is the greatest thing ever created? Love pervades and never harms anyone; people do.

Love Me For Me

Love me for me as I am all I have to give,

love me for me as I'll give you all that in me lives,

love me for me as I am all in - giving you my everything.

Love me for me as there is no pretence and all of me is what you see.

Love me for me as you are the one I adore & no one will ever love you more.

Love me for me as I see life's meaning through your eyes

and that love will remain until the day we die.

Love me for me as all I want is you &

I love you, for you;

Love me for me as I am love & love is me.

Sapiosexual

Your brilliance imprisons my thoughts and I get lost in the cleverness of your intellectual rapture, mental capture, tangled up in your clever—refusing to be released by one so gifted, whose smarts detain my senses and jail my attention indefinitely.

You're sharp, you're quick - Your witty meets mine and sends sparks to sensitive spaces and messages to ripe places and I am ready to collide and combust.

Talented genes, exceptional means; to express the simplest of things. Words so tantalizingly strung together that they leave me naught but my awe of you. Arrested by your outstanding, jailed by your excellence & compelled to accept only that which is incomparable to you.

Dazzled by you - controlled by my own
need to be drawn to your special,
I succumb to your power
over me, as my mind
romances yours and
I get lost in your
intelligent
you.

Mind-Massaging Conversations

I'd talk to you forever, without giving it a second thought;
you soothe me yet you excite me, you tickle my funny bone
and make me feel surrounded by you even when I'm all alone.

You make me smile even when I don't want to and you make me all warm and mushy inside. The wisps
of flirting that's so very sweet give me shy but sexy thoughts that makes me want to tap my feet.

I said it before but I'll say it again, I'd talk to you forever. Your words enslave me, they wrap
me deep inside a place where I never knew existed. Eyes forced closed by the timbre of your
voice, the power of your words and my need to simply listen as you speak.

Words so deep they floor me, sentences so profound they move me,
paragraphs of words laid out in such a way that they caress a mind now
made a slave to every letter of every word you speak.

My responses are automatic, in tuned to your every
word; I now hear you even before you speak. I
taste your words as they fall from your lips
and drip-drip-drip-drip all over the
most receptive parts of me. I
lose myself in them and we
both get lost in those
mind-massaging
conversations.

Heart-Juice

Squeezed of its juices, the heart strains to slow its own pace as it settles into a tempo of maddening beats that leaves you with less breath than an half-drowned fisherman.

Crammed against rib cages that are suffocating from the not so familiar closeness of a tick-ticker that is melted from the sheer presence of you, as you drain my heart of the natural juices that flow from the organ that keeps me alive, but that sometimes makes me wish I were dead; but not this time. As this time, my heart-juice is one made of the sweet nectar of romance—that smells of jasmine and entangled wisps - in a merger of scents so sweet you scarce can stand it.

Drained of its juices, the heart sighs deeply as it floats with precision to its destination where it grabs hold of whatever is deep inside, that space that has no choice but to be drawn to your….heart-juice.

It slithers its potent nectar into crevices & corners I had long forgotten and some I didn't even realize I had. Places that lay hopelessly unable to resist being devastatingly soaked by your….

heart-juice.

Time-Stop

Shifting waves that knock against a shore that welcomes them with outstretched hands - while their interplay brings them so irretrievably close - they become one. Lingering sunsets that hug a blue-black sky that kisses the atmosphere with the bliss of soon to be declared feelings that render time unnecessary in the face of emotions that encompass all that I am, or I ever hoped to be.

A mind entangled in a dance of uncertainty but safe in the knowledge that you want time to stay as is; never moving because yesterday is so far away and today is sweeter than anything you have ever known and better than anything that tomorrow could ever promise.

Lost in eyes so deep, I am taken into an abyss of the sweetest of revelations - when I am forced to explore why my heart is beating so hard against my chest and my brows are wet with perspiration of excitement while my heart sends messages to a brain that lays beautifully vulnerable to the mere presence of you.

Tomorrow is no longer important and yesterday holds no significance when all I now live for is right here - right now. I stare into the soul of the one who has given new meaning to my very existence; forever changing all that has ever happened before and rewriting what I previously believed to be my future.

My heart collided with the thrill that is you, and all I thought I knew became a shadow of what I now know, and life as I knew it ceased to exist because all I have ever wanted, but never even knew I did, is standing right across the room looking right back at me, in that unforgettable moment in my now wonderfully altered existence when time simply....

Stopped!!

11

You're My Every Moment

Trapped in the sweetest time-travel there is, when time ceases to move and I am stuck in the immovable wants I have and my need to possess every fiber of your being. Afraid to breathe as it threatens to remind me of the future when our bodies have to exit the place where we discovered our inability to live without each other so as to occupy two different geographical spaces, while our hearts and thoughts stay suspended; unable to move away from how we feel today and where we want to be forever.

Stuck in a time from which I am in no rush to escape as I relish being right here beside you, not wanting to be anywhere else, doing anything other than seeing and touching you, being with you as I am taken through the only thing I want to experience; existing in the same place where you are as your very existence stains my brain and engages my consciousness, while I soak up your aura and indulge in the essence of all that you are.

Existing in a space when the hands of the clock are merely a signal of the existence of time but gives no meaning to what really is of any importance to me since, I am transfixed in every moment that is sweetly & permanently marked by

Y.

O.

U.

12

You Are My Sunset

You are that beauty that can only be captured in the setting of the sun; when twilight meets the sky and explodes into wondrous visual ecstasy. You make my heart rest sweetly in the wonder of the exquisiteness that is imprisoned in the shadows that a disappearing sun casts on a once blue sea.

That contrast of dark and light that ignites a flame within me and makes me want to burn for you forever. That time-frame that has no ending; where beginnings have no meaning and a lifetime looms invitingly.

The promises of what is to come when the sun is finally gone to its temporary hiding place and I stand watching it disappear behind the clouds, giving me a reason to sigh in anticipation of its inevitable return.

You are beauty, you are bliss - I close my eyes in the rapture of you....my sunset.

13

Sweet "Somethings"

Listening keenly to whispered words that grab my attention and hold onto it with its powerful grip that I find impossible to escape. Thrilled by soft words that flow over sensitized skin and travel through pores opened - waiting for sexy words to be poured deep inside creamed ear drums.

Taken from places sane to spaces gone crazy with proclamations of thoughts that are inextricably enmeshed with discussion of feelings deeper than the ocean's floor - that swirl around in a head floating from a pressure point that's just too much for it to bear.

Terms coined from a heart filled with lust and spoken from a velvet tongue that is unable to contain the need to release what it knows to be real; expressions of a spirit buoyed by its own need to soar to reach its top-most point of articulacy. The involuntary communication of inner-most emotions made restless from enchanted minds that find it difficult to stay still.

A dialogue tainted with the residue of its own depth as it fails to wash away that which has held it captive for so much longer than it could ever imagine. Discourses that produce a secretion of oooohhhhssss and aahhhhssss, wrestled from places deep and otherwise taught to be untouchable.

Interchanges tangled up in honey dew, and marinated in sexy that leaves you hypnotized and lingering inside a sugar coma you never want to wake up from. Speeches from lips heavy with the nectar of succulent imaginings that stain the ears and capture senses that want to be imprisoned.

Statements of ownership from a barbaric need to enrapture and possess, with postulations of grandeur and the overwhelming need to ensnare your consciousness with vocal chords made wet from constant utterances of honey-flavoured bliss; that crescendos with a declaration that is saturated with the perfume of your oral emissions of "sweet somethings."

I Am Soooo Into You...

You intrigue me and I'm taken by your ability to hold my interest - a very difficult thing to do. You are the simple to my complex, the serene to my chaos - you calm my ruffled feathers and soothe my over-worked mind. It's like coming home after a rough day to clean sheets and hot chocolate with marshmallows. You mellow me out and smooth out my mental wrinkles; turning my frowns upside-down. You're the eye in my storm, the chill to my hectic, the sane to my madness.

I can let go and be all of me; my vulnerabilities are my strengths and my strengths are made even stronger when I'm around you. You bring out my softest and warmest sides, and make me happy to embrace all of me. You create for me an oasis, where I can rest my weary brain and feel cherished for more than a while. You make me feel so special and now I'm living in a forever smile.

I like best - the me I am with you; the calm me, the peaceful me, the sweet me, the me that wants to be just a girl to be pampered and spoiled. I like the me that you like, and I love the you- you are with me. I have to admit, I cannot pretend, as I always have to be honest with self - I'm so damn into you and I am SURE you knew, at least I HOPE you do?

The Rainy Sea

The pulsating, swelling, crescendo of tides that ebb and flow that push and pull and toss around; that set unclothed bodies on unsteady feet that heighten the wave's intensity and lend more 'rrrrr' to its roar. that wraps tightly and sheaths inside its unexpected warmth, souls left adrift that want to be so!!

Bodies crashing against each other, forced together by nature's will, but staying together through a resolve of their own; that tilt and shove and demand the attention of every fiber of the being, some willingly, others involuntarily.

Senses over-stimulated, curves caressed, kisses multiplied as bodies strain against each other to steady wobbly feet, and satisfy the need to be close while they feed off each other whilst nature melts into the natural need to purr and moan, when the rain meets the sea and creates in its wake - an electrifying explosion of feelings unmatched and even unmet; of impossible resistance to pulse-enhancing, hair-raising, heart-elevating, body-shivering, eyes-closing, lips-tingling, hips-moving, earth-shattering, controllable trembling of nerve-endings.

The rainy sea; the combined forces of elements that leave you simply....breathless!!

16

Island in the Sea

Waters of deep blue-green, melting into waves that beat upon white shores in the middle of an ocean floor. Bottomless stares melted into a heated desire to slide into nature's depths and immerse self into pores of wondrous ecstasy.

Moving to the beat of the rhythm reflected in your lover's eyes, as you draw him deep inside to a space that hosts life's sweetest nectar – as you transcend normal's realm to find a perch atop the bliss of a particular cloud; refusing to come down, as you struggle to hold onto scattered senses and runaway heartbeats that render you incapable of coherent thoughts.

The ocean's dance mixed with waves created by gyrating bodies wound tightly into their own sensual orchestra; of beats that shift blood flow to familiar areas that feel all new, and alter the tempo of each molecule of all that surrounds you.

No thought given to the possible demise from drowning, as living becomes secondary to a being transported to just feelings; where all rational thoughts are superseded by pleasurable sensations that trapeze from a swirling head to tingling toes.

Rapture un-curtailed & as raw as nature itself, as it finds its way to private places and makes happy spaces of contours and concaves that are built just for loving. Complete abandon, total oblivion to people, time and even place, as reality tries to seep its mundane way into glorious reality.

Rhapsody meets nature head on, in a race to greet satisfaction's pinnacle, and sweet release floats by, where the ocean meets the sky & where love was made, on an island in the sea….

I wanna Be Loved

I wanna be loved;
to be the subject of that look that threatens to melt the very air around me.
I wanna be loved;
to be the topic of a man's conversation that lights his eyes, ignites his smile and makes him animated.
I wanna be loved;
to walk away and know that he cannot wait for the day to end and for me to walk back into him arms.
I wanna be loved;
to be the first thing a man thinks about and the last thought he has before he drifts off to dreams of me.
I wanna be loved;
to be the future you are looking towards, the present you wanna live in and the past you always want to remember.
I wanna be loved;
to be your dream realized, your what you have always been looking for, the culmination of all you want your life to be.
I wanna be loved;
to be the light in your sunset, your rainbow after your rain, your refuge after a long day and your safe
place to retreat to when life gets too hard.
I wanna be loved;
to be the chocolate topping on your sundae, the icing on your cake, the cream on
your pie and the whip cream on your strawberries.
I wanna be loved;
to be the lyrics that you groove to, the thought that moves you,
and the things you're into.
I wanna be loved;
to be the one your heart beats for; you lick your
lips for, your eyes follow across the room;
the one who makes you think of
romance and happily ever
after.
I wanna be loved….
by you….

18

Mesmerized by You

Taken outside the ordinary and transported to a realm where things are capitalized and punctuated by things that can never be called mundane. Enthralled by your ability to take my mind somewhere my body doesn't even recognize; drawing from me, an involuntary response to all your intentions to take me "there."

Fascinated by you and taken aback by your charm that has me second-guessing my own resolve and wondering at my incapacity to say no to anything you want from me. Awestruck by your moves, your groves, your ability to own a room, as your natural gait makes heads swivel and hearts quiver.

Rapt attention paid to you, as mere mortals cannot comprehend the depth of your swagger. Drawing from minds their complete wonder - of a you pervaded in splendor. Captivated by the aura of you - as you saturate my tame senses into thinking wayward thoughts and moved to touch you as if by compulsion while my thoughts work overtime in its futile attempt to curtail my actions.

Enchanted by the mere presence of you, the essence of you, and the core of who you are; my mind is propelled into thinking thoughts no one can call pure; wondering, waiting, needing, having feelings I struggle to comprehend. So enthralled by the very "you-ness" of you that I'm finding it impossible to dig my way from beneath elevated heartbeats and uncontrolled breathing, made so by my ineffectual attempts at moving my thoughts away from what is my new obsession.

Engrossed in trying to temper my excitement at just the thought and mere sight of you; telling myself that I can conquer my runaway thoughts—rein them in to redirect their path to think on other things; things that used to be significant but have now been greatly diminished in comparison to the thoughts I have of you.

Mesmerized by You continued

I'm gripped by way too much charisma that seeps through my every pore, permeating every single fibre of every little part of me. Fighting to calm pulsating energies in places I didn't even knew existed, unable to distinguish between where my thoughts stop and my feelings begin, as I try without success, to give meaning to all that this is.

I'm absorbed by you; your un-orchestrated way of pulling me into the depths of you. Soaked in the you that is you, dripping of you; becoming weak with my need to bleed from the deepest insides of me – some of you, so some of me can remain to sustain the now willingly weaker side of my being that has been captured by you.

Wrapped up in my need to tie myself even more inextricably to you, bonding me even closer to everything about you; I'm melting inside you, becoming ingrained in your make-up, so you are unable to escape me in the same way escaping you is impossible for me. Immersed totally, all of me; mind, body and soul in your feel, your taste; the aroma of you, as I exhale, but only so I can have the capacity to breath you in again & again.

Completely draped in the sensation that is you, the work of art that I view; I struggle to find me, since all I ever seem to see, is you.

Riveted to you as a moth to those irresistible flames - finally giving in to what I have always known to be true, that I am - charmed, enchanted, fascinated, captivated; just utterly mesmerized by you.

20

Inside Your Hug

It's my FAVOURITE place to be;

all warm and snugly— the only parts left un-hugged are those places where your arms cannot presently encircle me.

It's my SAFEST place to be;

all secured in your arms that are embracing me: pulling me close to your chest as your heart beats against mine.

It's my WARMEST place to be;

all happy and contented as I relish in the coziness I feel when I am engulfed in your liquid tenderness while I watch as your enjoyment mirrors mine.

It's my HAPPIEST place to be;

when I am all giggly, and silly and carefree with a my mind open and receptive to a simple, yet powerful unspoken human expression of affection. When I am wrapped up in your hug, it is more than just an action, it's the definition of a reciprocally loving reaction that involuntarily closes eyes, emits sighs and creates automatic heart smiles.

Wistful Longings

Contemplative and soft they are, as they take flight from the conscious realm and move into the imaginary where endless longing never ends. They touch, then they go, leaving behind them trails of heavenly longing as you perceive their presence, vibe with their wanting, settle deep inside their wistful stares while they stay away....just outside your grasp.

He's right there you can almost touch him; his sinewy muscles bulging as big as your eyes with his aura so potent, you hide sighing smiles as smells mix with the raw power of the unknown and you think back on those days when your fantasies should have remained untried as you now realize that wishing for was so much better than knowing, as knowing did not live up to your imaginings....until now.

She's there inside your scope of touch; sitting perched upon those erotic tingling of things to come that are way too potent to ignore. Adrift goes your mind, down paths winding upwards those pinnacles that leave your imagination struggling to come down from clouds way beyond nine. She's so close by, but albeit she's just a touch away from fulfilling those recurring dreams; she's always just a step outside your grasp....

Outside your grasp; just staying long enough to stain a mind that can never forget -stopping for a while but never staying for too long, flitting through thoughts that wish you would stay and leave trails of remembering where continuity is absent as it lacks staying-power - but it teases you un-mercilessly since she never goes away.

Beautiful and unforgettable; journeying from place to place - present but never staying for too long. You can perceive and even touch them but you can never hold on. That's the reality of those life-changing, yet fleetingly wistful moments, when you have to temporarily let go of the dream of love that presently is, but will not be forever unrequited.

Cuddle Partner

STRONG, **WARM** arms, circling my **SOFTNESS**
as your sweet breath caresses the back of my neck.
I turn to cradle my head in the crook of your arms,
while I lay my leg lazily across yours.

Your chin lays softly on the top of my head
as you tenderly rub my temples. Oh
the many aromas of you & the hardness of a body
that draws from me a longing sighhhhhhhh....

I snuggle even deeper,
you hold me even tighter....
and I drift off into dreams sweet
with my extremely sexy...
cuddle partner.

Sweet Torture

Pain and Pleasure wrapped so tightly together; imbedded inextricably into each other, that you have to fight to distinguish between the two. One starts so effortlessly where the other left off; you cannot decide whether to laugh or to cry since you want it to stop but need it to continue.

Is it pain? is it pleasure? or is it the miraculous combination of the two? Am I hurting? am I in bliss, please tell me which is it. I cannot stop to figure it out; will the cessation of the pain stop the pleasure? What have I discovered, is it torture or a priceless treasure?

Enmeshed polarity converged in complexity; creating twin-peaks of sensations that are bounded way too tightly to become separated; pondering if there will be a tempering of the bliss that you are so reluctant to relinquish.

Entangled divergence, not caring to be released; from the contradicting sensations that are such sweet torture.

Sun Showers

Bright rays with the ability to over-power—
but step back to complement sweet-smelling showers
in a blend of liquid-sunshine, bleeding its way down
willing vices - all ripe and ready to bellow softly
into moments of pleasure that know no tomorrow.

Pretty streaks of sunbeams, shining through glass-colored raindrops,
that beat on streets of rain-bowed treasures -
that move towards pools of warm-rain;
waiting to meet up with each other.

Inter-twined layers of hot and cold;
of sun and rain, of bright and dark -
forces combined to release warm thunder;
cool lightening, sunny rain, all coming together
to receive nature's wonderful confusion.

Rainbows formed in puddles of rainy heat -
escaping to places unseen. Cold heat raining
down on lovers' heads - wanting to run for
cover, yet standing still,
as their feet are reluctant to
leave behind,
beauty so undefined.

Hhhhmmmm...That Voice

Deep timbers of resonance; echoing through strands that hold nerve-endings—sending shivers down a spine left weak from the inability to comprehend what the brain wants the legs to do.

A mind taken from the zone of comfort and blasted into the realm of ohhhhhhs and ahhhhhhs - blistered by thoughts unrefined and impure - ready to twist words into actions of things so sweet they are indescribable.

"Gasmic vibings," cerebral dancing; the urge to chant from a space of wanting. Pimples of the "goose" kind, a tingling that threatens to blow the mind. Sly smiles of delayed gratification captured in the whimsy of the knowledge of what could be, all wrapped up in the voice behind the man - making me want to plaster it against throbbing ears, so as to set unmentionable places ablaze.

HHHMMMM....that Voice....

Cerebral Seduction

It starts in the mind - that mental stimulation that keeps the brain cells pulsating to their very own rhythm, and jiving to their own sensual beats. The capturing of that space in my head that is hardly touched so that it goes into utter shock from the caressing of its pinnacle.

My brain does its victory jig: welcoming the action it deems entirely necessary to get it out of its self-induced coma, as it rolls off its lazy perch to respond to what has now become the master of its destiny.

The inside of my cranium is being bled of its restraint, and I am hypnotically led into strands of sweetness by quivering thoughts and shivering imaginings - surrendering to depths of sensations that have rendered my legs..liquid.

Silent Eloquence

It speaks so loudly with no actual words to penetrate the *articulate* silence that sweetly surrounds us. Your ability to speak oh so *clearly* with just one look, a *soft* touch, a hint of a smile that speaks *volumes* to the most sensitive side of me. My intuitiveness has been heightened to discern what your look, your touch and your sultry smile mean, since my heart involuntarily responds to your loudest of silence.

Words have *no* place in moments made so *perfect* by souls en-twined and spirits linked together in the sweet knowledge of our unspoken needs. The mood, the breeze, the ambiance, the meshed spirits and the kindred souls are the only sounds necessary to create the dialogue of two hearts so in-tuned to each other that mere words are not needed for the expression of the depth of love being shared. Yet love is so clearly expressed; punctuated by such silent eloquence.

Love Trumps all

It's bigger than words
larger than life
the greatest high
the biggest thrill
the tallest height
the deepest depth
the strongest feeling
the most profound meaning
the superglue
the honey dew
the brightest sun
the best of the crop
the cherry on top
the "in" in origin
the "h" in hot
the hit spot
the reason your heart skips beats,
your knees get weak &
life as you know it changes
forever!!

The Blushing Sky

Its magnificent blue winks at you, as you take me in your arms and kiss my lips ever so lightly, I wonder if it really happened.

The stars twinkled as my cheeks dimpled—my smile enveloping yours while the moon dims, offering us its intimate privacy that cocoons the love that radiates and punctuates a sky that is eager to embrace it.

The clouds dip low, swirling over our joined lips; whispering of its sweetness; making the galaxy pale in comparison.

The universe tries to compete but is left wanting,
as the sky blushes while it watches two of
earth's occupants melt into each
other and become one.

Saturation

Heart aflutter, mind blown, lips tingly just from looking at your luscious two—
praising the gods that you are my boo.

Loins tingling, juices mingling, thoughts transcended to plains uncharted and
yet to be scaled.

Immersed in you, reversed dew—mists that get soaked up long before
they hit the ground; getting scorched by the heat of you. Joy
quadrupled, happy super magnified & synergy achieved, as all of
me soaks up all of you and the world spins out of control,
when I breathe you in and exhale you through
my every pore, seeping through myself and
melting deliciously into you.

Love Is...

- when knowing you feels like forever, as you know me like no other
- when loving you is easier with every breath i take
- when my soul spreads it wings and welcomes you in
- when the stars twinkle in sweet conspiracy
- when the sun shines its glee
- when the moon smiles its willing approval.
- when my heart speaks in a language that only your heart hears
- when life seems so much brighter
- my journey is so much lighter
- when love has finally found its true meaning
-when your beginning is my end & your end begins me

love is....

y.o.u.

Dedicated to the love of Judith & Raymond

32

Love Unfettered

Unencumbered by intentions, influenced only by sweet reciprocation, moved by its own bidding to do what it does so well, all on its own.

Acting from a place of unselfishness, confident in the knowledge that love knows no bounds, and guided into the truth of what it really is about.

When you say those three big words; the biggest three strung together— they should come with no cost, no conditions or trappings of obligation. They are free from isms, never altered or shrouded by schisms, and far removed from all agendas hidden.

Unchanged by time, unmoved by someone else's inability to be loved just for who they are. Uplifted in its own magnificence as it takes its rightful perch a-top the word list - as love is love, and cannot be usurped.

It is never changing, cause when love is true, there's no substitute, no falling out of, no games and no taking it back. You dance, you skip, ignoring little scrapes and nips, as you know you will be ok when you love someone true.

When someone loves you - with a love that is unfettered; unbothered by cynicism, it will be, now and forever, the sweetest truth you will ever know.

Hidden in Plain View

A quiet strength that's not screaming "pick me, pick me." A persona that's charming without being overwhelming; a force that doesn't bellow but that is not to be reckoned with.

A mind of steel, a resolve to be whatever you want to be. Resolute in who you are without the accompaniment of bells and whistles. A jewel in your own right; hidden right there in plain sight….there for all to see if they look hard enough - a potency that is hardly ever experienced - yet when it has been, it cannot be mistaken.

Hidden right there in the plain view, for those discerning enough to see. Your power, your grace, your charm, your sense of who you are; all seen without lighted arrows pointing to it.

Your light shines brighter because it's so visible even though it is shining from so far back from all the glitz & pageantry. It's so much louder as it doesn't need to shout to be heard, so much sweeter, as its shimmer and its shine are more lasting than those spotlights that burn out after just a little while.

You're a gem, and I'm happy to have discovered you, even while you were still hidden in plain view.

Scented Moments

Perfumed milliseconds 'tick-tocking' slowly by, in reverence of my awe of you & me. Fragrant minutes dragging along; delaying my soon to be reluctant absence from your presence.

Pungent hours; stained with my longing to possess you and keep you forever mine, Aromatic days, swollen with companionship so sweetly sustained by the need to be a part of something that takes more than just needs to keep it afloat.

Piquant months, made savory with ripe desire and satisfied loins.
Spicy years of contentment and appreciation for what was, is & yet to be,
coupled with odorous decades 'stenched' with memories you want to
keep with you for longer than forevermore.

Sweetness resonating so loudly it splatters against
the insides of me & shatters my half-hearted
resistance to you and I am left with
memories of seconds, minutes.
hours, days, months, years
and decades I could
never forget, even
if I tried.

The Unveiling

Strip me of my reservations ; remove from me my cloak of innocence as I gravitate to you with no will of my own. Unclothe me of my inhibitions, leave me naked and panting for something I know I want yet unsure of what it is.

Disrobe my longings and robe me with a knowledge so raw that it takes my breathe away. Lay me bare of my needs and wrap them up in opulence and greed and leave me temporarily satiated but always ready for more.

Divest my most valuable belongings and instead, pervade me with a feeling so blissful there is no scope for containment. Uncover my deepest me and expose it to your lingering explorations that end my conscious thoughts yet prolong them in my subconscious me.

Strip me of all my reticence so that I can be free to reveal to you, my innermost me. Unveil me, set me f.r.e.e to obsessively return to those 'wantings' that now permanently stain me, leaving on me, the eternal mark of you.

The Kiss

The right amount of tongue, just enough moisture, the tilting of heads, the laboured breaths, the intermittent groans, the thump-thumping of hearts, the heaving of erotic parts.

The change in temperature, the wetting of spaces, the aroused places, the butterflies in the stomach and the one wanting to melt into the other. Breaths tingling, tongues intermingling, bodies entwined, lips locked, arms inter-locked; behind heads that have long forgotten where I begin and where you end.

Thoughts wayward, feelings mixed-up, with shivers down spines, quivers divine, sugary lips and pointy tips; tongues dancing their own 'lil 'jig, and you get lost in sensations so sweet it's almost unbearable.

Eyes shut tight, the pressure's just right, toes curled and caution gets thrown to the wind. Involuntary moans, body parts now hard as stones - as lips stay locked, brains cells get out of whack and you become deliciously transcended.

Romance Me...

I'm a simple girl with girly wishes, wanting flowers, candy and butterfly kisses. My roses don't have to be red, they can be pink or yellow too, and I so want to share some moonlight moments with you.

Call me just to say hi, send me a card just because....hug me just to hold me with nothing else on your mind. I like quiet moments, long drives, us holding hands, with walks along lonely-lonely beaches with bare feet touching sand.

Candle light in romantic spaces, where hearts speak and joy is felt in unusual places. Take me on a gondola ride, look deep into my eyes & tell me sweet 'somethings' that mean nothing to others, but mean the world to me. Make me laugh with head thrown back, be sweet to me so I can keep these feelings forever bundled up in my love sack.

The little things are what move me, that make me happy. A smile, a hug, a word sweetly said, as that is what usually gets stuck in my head. Kiss my hand, rub my feet, engage the confines of my mind, give me a flower for no reason and smile at me like it's smiling season. Engage my intellect, caress my brain cells; take care of my mind, and my body will be more than happy to eventually take care of you.

You – My Rain

The sound – that pitter-patter that lulls my soul to complete peace; that lends itself to sighs infinite; that creates a litany of feelings so calming, I am melting through myself.

The smell; freshness personified, captured in continuous drops of liquid silk that touch the earth and create its own amalgamation of perfumed reality; that leave me spellbound - wanting to freeze time.

The imagery it conjures up; that space of cuddliness; of wanting to be hugged and made love to; to be taken away on rapture's wings - as I float away to sweet imaginings. Moved to close my eyes and be whisked away to a place where the rain is captured in a never-ending song.

You - my rain; capturing all it encompasses and thrusting me against my innermost me; intense, connected, in tuned, captivated, renewed and ready to infiltrate all of me with all of you.

The Idea of You

I think of you; thoughts not yet purposeful; but are nevertheless lingering as my mind tries to center itself on the idea of you. I think of you too, thoughts that not yet stain my guarded brain, but consider the probability of you.

It stakes no claim on you; makes no demands of you but if allowed, my mind would seize the opportunity to pounce on the suggestion of you. You stay on the outskirts of a mind that prefers to wait and see, while still holding pleasant thoughts of you; testing the mental waters of you; skirting around the if, the maybe; the likelihood of you.

My cautious mind beckons brain cells to think thoughts of you, impressing upon me the need to allow my mind to wonder, think, ponder; until it gets to that juncture, when time brings me to an answer as to the possibility of you.

The Heart's Last Call

It shuts its door, but it's not locked, even though hurt has rendered it temporarily out of service. It ignores near misses, skirts around close calls and shields itself in emotional bubble-wrap. Wrapped up in steel-like cloaks, it dodges Cupid's arrows – breaking them into tiny little pieces and throwing them into wells— way deep.

Love? What exactly is that? it asks angrily of the ones knocking-knocking at its door. It impatiently waits as disgust takes forever to close that gate, where love stands mockingly inside. My heart's door is shut, it screams from its gut, as it feels its resolve shaking.

Leave me alone; loud is its groaning — the closer it gets to giving in. Resistance crumbling, heart again up and running, but caution is the name of the game. You have a sick sense of humour it retorts, as it glares daggers at a head that is telling it that a closed heart never finds love.

Love? what exactly is that? It asks again, but this time a lot less angry, as it smiles weakly at its latest interest. OK, OK, I GIVE IN, it bellows, as it answers its last call; albeit just a tad appalled – when love finally found its way back home.

41

Just Us, Just Now...

No pretense
no holding back
no over-thinking
no impossibilities
no awkward moments
no pregnant pauses
no excess words.

No worries about the future
no thoughts about tomorrow
no hurry to be anywhere but here
no rush to say goodbye
nu rush to get 'there.'

No flights to take
no meetings to make
no points to prove
nothing to loose
it's just you, just me, just here,
just now,
just us.

Maybe...

Maybe you're in my head, maybe you're not, maybe for a change I will welcome my bed so I can dream of things that may turn into something hot. I don't rule things out, or even try to think ahead. Instead , I leave my mind opened to things that are left to be said. Possibilities of the endless kind; I live and breathe for those, as I smile my own 'l'il' secret smiles and wait for whatever the universe bestows.

Patience has never been my strong suit, but if it's worth it, waiting is something I can do I suppose. Maybe I want you -maybe I don't, maybe I'll tell you - if I found out or maybe I won't. But if feelings get to be too much for my silence, then I'd definitely tell you and we'll see how it goes.

Maybe I'm falling for you, maybe that's true, maybe you will reciprocate if you have those same feelings too; oh if only I knew. Look closely, peer deep into my eyes and that window will be wide opened and perhaps you will see that maybe it's true that I do dig you, maybe....

Melodic Whispers

Candy-covered lyrics saturated with the sweetest of sounds; not amplified, just whispered into ears perked up and more than ready to listen. I wait every day; not too patiently - just to be whispered to by a voice that deliciously relieves me of my usual calm.

Even in a whisper it is loud — not in volume, but in its ability to engulf me so completely. It sounds like music up- in -here, even though you're not even singing, and your voice is the only instrument being played.

Orchestra-like rhythms floating over eardrums that wait impatiently; willing you to speak to them in that way that only you can. You whisper to me in melody; fine-tuning those sultry vocal cords and wooing me with that silver tongue in a tone so low that only I can hear.

And as I twist and turn to get into that perfect position, I wait with bated breath trying to teach myself to be always in-tuned to your melodious whispers.

Love's Cost

Can you buy it, bribe it. demand it. deny it
can you REALLY????

Can you resist it, justify it, validate it. force it
can you REALLY??

Can you cajole it. trick it, lie to it. lie for it
can you REALLY?

Can you hide from it. die from it. stay away from it. do without it
can you REALLY?

Can you beg for it. refuse to give it. get enough of it
can you REALLY????

No you can't as it is free, unbounded
kind, needed, necessary & given
without measure 'cause the
cost of love, is love.

Chemistry

Brain smiles: broadened by the presence of chemistry undefined and undeniable. One man, one woman: engaged in the timeless, unrehearsed dance of "chem-traction" – chemistry intertwined with hard to ignore attraction.

Hands so huge; yet so soft – my mind's eyes close when they engulf mine. Heart laughs; at the sexy humour of a conspiring universe that is busy working in our favour - even when we have no idea what is to come but are gamed for its revelation.

"Stalkingly" close: coincidences that aren't really all that coincidental, as again the cosmos wink knowingly at its live bates; mere mortals who are playing right into its hands. Giddy school girl laughter; more than a hundred text messages - signaling something too profound to mix in a Pyrex dish in some remote science lab somewhere "out there."

It's chemistry baby – words written after written words harmonize and inhabit the atmosphere simultaneously. Naughty thoughts, tantalizing imaginings wrought, as heartbeats increase, minds get creamed and the stage is set for infinite romantic possibilities.

Love-Wrecked

Derailed from all coherent thoughts, my mind overturns any way of thinking that is not in synch with what my body wants from you.

Overturned resistance; pushed aside for the madness that threatens to rage out of control; yes rage, RAGE, and capsize my cool equilibrium. Turn it upside down & inside out; wreak havoc with my brain, as it topples over itself in its haste to retreat from the intensity that's taking over, leaving it powerless and weak in its wake.

A collapsed heart; deflated in its audacity to think it could resist your captivating pull and stop its tumble from grace as it catapults unceremoniously into your deliberately placed web of rapture.

Soul upended
resolve drained
pride squeezed dry
resistance smashed -
since life as I know it has been
re-routed, cause I'm now
unstoppably &
hopelessly….love-
wrecked.

Lust's Trail

Pathway slivered with things that wet lips and doubly stimulate splits in covered up spaces. Tracks made slippery with thoughts not readily revealed in fear of its shock effect. Roadways permanently stained by the sweat that drains off writhing bodies; rapturously joined and straining to stay that way.

Footpaths marked by the "X" in ecstasy that renders you breathless yet you never want to breathe again if your next breath will alter your present state of being. A thoroughfare not frequented by this depth of desire that takes you to heights unparalleled and forces you onto dangerous highways and winding byways that leave your head spinning and your loins tingling.

Narrow lanes that feel even smaller as your chest constricts and your heart pumps away at too many miles per hour, so you sprint to the back alley to escape unbearable sweetness that leaves nerve endings raw, that become conduits of flowing juices that end up in channels deep and corridors that freely open up to let bliss have its own way.

Hallways of pure, unadulterated lust that offers unending release to insatiable feelings that run rampant through a body that lays prostrate—offering itself up as an access strip for all things pleasurable, as it trails its way into damp, darkened places, made hard and elongated by its greed to explode into a kaleidoscope of sensations that relieve the body of its strength and the mind of its ability to think coherently.

Lust's trail, the direct route to cloud nine.

The Magic of Y.O.U.

Bells ringing, but I only hear them inside my head as it excites at the sight of you. Butterflies have found their way into my previously calm stomach as I watch you coming closer and closer to me. I want to flee from feelings so intense and new, yet instead I stand there transfixed, not knowing what to do.

Common sense taking flight and I think—maybe it's not so wise after all, but there I go again, instead of fleeing, I stand there seeing....life as I know it disappears right before my very eyes. I still have time enough to flee, before all of you captures all of me, and I am even more far gone than I already am. So, I made my move, but found myself running to meet you, as if pulled by some invisible string into outstretched waiting arms, while the rest of me collides with the holder of my heart, in an embrace that leaves me wondering just where you end and where I start.

No abracadabra, no hocus-pocus, no disappearing rabbits or none of that fuss. Just love's potency doing what it does best; taking a heart from its owner and putting it to rest – in the hands of someone whose heart I also now hold to cherish, since it's more precious than gold. The mystery has ended; there was no need to flee, as I look up from our tight embrace, into a face mirroring my glee. If this is magic, I pray nothing disappears, as my search for love is over and I have conquered my fears.

Butterfly Moments

Wistful and soft they are as they take flight from the conscious realm –and move into the imaginary, where endless longings never end. They touch, then they go; leaving behind their trails of blissful wanting as you perceive their presence, vibe with their taunting, settle deep inside their wistful stares while they stay away….just outside your grasp.

He's right there you can almost touch him; his sinewy muscles bulging as big as your eyes become from staring. His aura so potent, you hide 'sighing' smiles— perfumed visuals mixed with the raw power of the unknown, as you think back on those days when your fantasies should have remained untried, when wishing for was so much better than knowing, and knowing did not truly live up to your imaginings.

She's there inside your nearest grasp, sitting perched upon those erotic tingling of things to come that are way too potent to ignore. Adrift goes your mind, down paths winding upwards to those pinnacles that leave it struggling to come down. She's right there, but albeit she's just a touch away from fulfilling those recurring dreams –she's always just a step outside even the closest of close you've managed to achieve.

Outside my grasp; staying just long enough to stain a mind that can never forget. Stopping for a while but never staying too long - flitting from thoughts that wish you would stay & leaving trails of remembrance where continuity is absent - lacking in staying-power, yet never truly leaving.

Beautiful and unforgettable Journeying from place to place, coming by but never lingering. You can perceive and even touch them but can never hold unto them for time--extended, 'cause that's just how it is - those life-changing, yet delightfully fleeting …butterfly moments.

Heart Work

Pumping, pumping - moving blood to places brought to my attention by sensations that simply refuse to quit. Giving life to ripened thoughts - waiting to be expressed through the thump-thumping of arteries that give life, and veins that carry from place to space; meanings of ecstasy unexplained.

Deafening beats giving sounds to unspoken thoughts buoyed and ricocheting all over valves that work overtime to keep in pace with thoughts that are running away from me.

Thump-pity thump is all I can hear, as I struggle against my better judgment to simply throw caution to the wind and with my everything; simply jump right in. Heart smiles, broad "ticker" grins, memories too sweet, no time for chagrin.

No thoughts are necessary, logics be damned, I forget about tomorrow, as right now is all I need to understand. My brain is pouting as I have no time to feed it, since all energies are riveted on a place that ticks, ticks, ticks and yes....ticks.

This work of heart, this mobilization of my ticker and those cherished moments, when you set my heart a flicker-to beat out of my chest, those unsaid feelings lying within my breast, my body comes alive in its great expectations of what is to come.

With a pump, and a beat, this thumpity thump is all I can think with. It sways me, it curtails me & holds me, but yet it sets me free, so my heart can work its way right to the doorstep of the one I am destined to leave the other piece of my heart with.

Sweet Talk

Drenched and still dripping; made wet from words filled with liquid warmth that gives a pulse to places that should not have a heart but that beat as if they do. Forbidden feelings, frowned upon thoughts made no less potent by convention and manmade boundaries that have no place in ecstasy's realm. Where romance is more important than dreams, and love takes center stage; negating anything as mundane as common sense and the 'norm.'

Anticipation that surpasses anything that reality can offer to a soul that wants you so badly it becomes a need that has to be satisfied, or life no longer makes any kind of sense, and I would rather be absent from the present than live without your words that have me spellbound and hopelessly lost in my need to listen to nothing else but you.

I transcend my usual, am taken away from my normal to float above life's commonplace and am propelled into a space that is out of this world; that sets my mind in high gear, my body in overdrive, my thoughts beyond the ordinary and all my senses wrapped up and tangled up in everything your lips do and say.

I hear you, I absorb your words that saturate my very soul and leave me unable to keep control over the pattern of my own breathing, as the words you string together are no longer just words, but sentences transformed into enchantment with the ability to move me into a sphere where magic lives, love has a different meaning and I am nothing means anything if you're not there.

For N & J, CIL

52

Heart Strokes

Rubbing sensitive places, taking mental back flips, stroking pointy tips - as you wait to strip yourself of useless inhibitions. Your mind is keenly attuned to the thump-thumping of blood being pumped around to sensitive hot spots that have a heart of their own, as they beat in the rhythm of those hhhhmmmms and ahhhhs that are waiting for their toe-curling finale.

Slipping special parts into ripen, throbbing sections created to sheath rods of warmth that sets your insides a-flicker - stroking your blood pumper as it beats a thousand miles per hour – recognizing its own power to further mesmerize a mind already blown away and a body that is now a slave to you.

Butterfly kisses on candy-covered crevices that are ready to receive from its giver. 'Breast strokes' abound, eyes buried in curvy mounds, lips properly licked to its perfect plump, as the heart continues its 'thumpity-thump' while you wait impatiently for the sweetest of conclusions.

Where The Sun Meets The Sea

A sphere of 'in-between-ness'
in-between pleasure and absolute harmony
where colours collide
and yellows and blues dance in synchrony -
cancelling out the black that my heart used to be.

*Peeking from beneath swollen candy-white clouds; plumped and teased by the warmth
of you — reflecting its rays of ecstasy on the liquid heaven that lies beneath it —
caressingly lit by the radiance of it. Resplendent in its own regal dress but
made even more so by your special glow.*

We laugh, we kiss, we hug, we dismiss….all the things
that just do not fit as we sweetly float upwards —
suspended in time, where the sun meets
the sea, somewhere out there, where
life's in-betweens have never
been this blissful.

54

Walking On Air

Floating – feet unable to hold me up as I'm suspended in time—perched on the edge of feelings that are about to propel me into uncharted realms—balanced on beams of delight.

Hovering over something that is bigger than me, while I wait on the brink of contentment that is finally within my reach—that lays on that edge of profound feelings and threatens to blow me away as I hang by the thread of my near-desperation to be with you.

Looking down from my vantage point, I throw my head back in flirty laughter at the joy reflected in eyes that are stayed on me; lightheaded and happy, giddy with glee.

I smile at you sweetly - watching you begin your own ascent to join me, in that place where love has us both…. walking on air.

I Miss You When...

I have to close my eyes to sleep

I Miss You When....

I stop to take my next life-sustaining breath

I Miss You When....

I blink and my eyes pause to look at you again

I Miss You When....

I am not able to think my sexy thoughts of you

I Miss You When...

You go too deeply into yourself that I cannot find you

I Miss You When....

The stars blinks and I temporarily lose sight of you

I Miss You When....

My arms are empty and I cannot hold you

I Miss You When....

Life's sweetness engulfs me and the world's
joy surrounds me, as even my sweetest
existence gets over-shadowed in a
kaleidoscope of colours that
explode in my head - when
I am in the presence
of you....

56

Heart Jar

Overflowing with heart salve—waiting to be replenished with out-of-this-world feelings of rapture packed tightly with goose-pimply sensations - that make my vulnerable skin your willing playground.

Spilt bliss — splashing in ecstasy's clutches & covered in cookie-like sweetness that saturates my pores, rendering me even sweeter for you.

My lips smile almost involuntarily as I think of being surrounded by you — smothered in the heat that's you, in a space too tight for three, but just perfect for you & me.

Our heart jar — storage for a state
of being that pours from
a place that bleeds
l.o.v.e.

Beyond Infinity

Infinity's beyond
beyond forever
forever's never-ending
ending not
not ever
everlastingly lasting
lasting for always
always here
here eternally
eternally yours
yours forevermore
forevermore locked
locked intertwiningly
intertwiningly unbroken
unbroken connections
connections endless
endlessly yours
because beyond infinity
is how long
i will love you

Listen To My Heart

No words necessary, I 'feel' you loud & clear. Let me close my eyes and soak up the essence of you. Your heart speaks to mine and I am moved by the articulacy of their agreement as they communicate more profoundly than any words that our lips could ever say.

Ignore my shallow words, spurted from selfish lips instead of from a pure place; where my heart sits up and takes center stage and words become redundant.

Pay scant attention to my stubbornness to capture your attention by the sway of my hips and the pouting of my lips, when a level of communicating exists that is far deeper; that comes from a place where feelings are never misplaced and time is never of the essence, as haste is not even a factor.

Rest your head right there; yes, right between the valleys of my mounds and identify each beat as they create rhythms for your ears only; rhythms that move you even closer to me.

Listen to my heart and tell me what it says, as sometimes I misread its meanings and lose the essence of its messages in my haste to translate.

Listen to my heart, hear what it says and use its beats to dilute the noise of those unnecessary words that hold no real meaning.

She Is...

Mesmerizing she is....

Her words come from a place so pure, they go directly to your heart. They are not heard as much as they are felt. She is contradicting, a sly confidence - a simple, complex being, so hard yet as soft as an unintended kiss...

She is love...

I feel it from a place unexpected, without reason, by chance and without gimmick. It's driven from many facets, none more important than the other.

It's nice....a quiet sun shining through leaves type of feeling....It's a soothing, gentle patter of rain on a roof, with a rhythm so in tuned - adding to the symphony that is her.

She is guarded, yet free - stubborn yet listens and selfish with what's hers, but when she shares, it's heaven... it's special and she knows....

She is.... Camille

A cherished piece written for me – not by me

Love-Napped

Taken away from myself; I am left with no fight in me.
No resistance left as I give in to the pull of you - to be full of you.
Drawn into you- my thoughts all wrapped up in you, unable to take themselves off of you. Transfixed –
my mind is stayed on you; I'm stuck like glue, incapable of pulling myself away from you.

My senses so attuned to you, I become obsessed with you; my brain cells tingle for you. My heart
beats for you, my attention is fixed on you, I smell you, I taste you, I feel you, I see you – in
everything I do. You're my muse, my inspiration, the reason my next breath is taken.
You're my arousal, my expectation, my looking forward to; you're my meaning.

Captured by you, saturated by you, sinking into you - as all of me,
takes all of you and I lose myself in you. I no longer belong
to me; my heart stolen by you – never to be returned
to me.

I'm love-napped & hopelessly
unable to stop myself from
falling in love – with
you.

Love's Cycle

Snuggled beneath its circular warmth, I feel wrapped tightly in the promise of you. Nestled into a ball of fiery flame that threatens to explode into minute pieces of sweetness that penetrates my soul and gives love a brand new meaning.

Cuddled up so close that we are one to the naked eyes that are unable to see where I begin and you end. Circled by a force bigger than us, rendering two of the strongest people unable to win against its unyielding force. Nuzzled by this tantalizing love-source, we take our separate breaths, but in synchrony as we breath each other in.

Cozy nights, and even cozier days, spent together too lost in each other to care even if the world no longer existed after we exit our space of reverie. Clasped in embraces that pull us closer than crazy glue, I am as stuck on you as you on me and we embrace it all. Hugged by the most powerful of four letter words ever written by man but created by a force greater than any of us could ever comprehend.

Clutched by love's far-reaching tentacles, we worship at love's feet, incapable of saying no to its irresistible pull. Gripped by something tantamount to awe, but much bigger than we can even give meaning to. As love has clinched our hearts, stolen our minds and blew us so far out of the water that we are floating – elevated above ourselves, as our souls find each other where love goes to stay - forever.

Reverie

With my eyes to the stars, my back placed firmly on the sand – trancelike, transported, I am taken to that place where wonder resides. Daydreams abound – too much to not be taken in and away from the mundane and transported to rapture's hunting ground where dreams are so real you can touch them.

Trance-like states inhabited by a you – you have never met, with musings so outside of your normal, you try to wrap your head around the magnitude of them. Fantasy's house invaded by the newly-found you, as you try to steal from the universe, its power to encircle everything all at once.

Head in the clouds, floating above its usual sphere, finding its way to the place your heart has been expelled to – beyond seventh heaven, just outside of beyond the ninth cloud.

Spells casted, dazed by wonderment that is out of this world - and even outside the scope of those you've ever imagined.

stupor

reflection

meditation so deep you are incapable to pulling yourself away from the stain that is left on your soul by something you cannot wash away even if you tried. Thoughts centered on one thing – that thing that is sought by all, found by some but needed by all to make the world as it should be.

Ponderings and wonderings – a mind blown,
a heart captured, and a body way
beyond ready to be skyrocketed to
ecstasy's realm – unwilling
to return to what
was, as what is
- is so much
sweeter.

Scented Candle Light

The soft flicker, hidden just beyond itself, capturing you at your softest, bouncing your perfect reflection off the wall and onto a me that is suddenly a fool for you. That scented warmth reverberated around my wayward senses, tantalizing and alluringly trapping me into a spell I never want broken – ever. I think not of escape but of pulling even closer to its subtle invite as I become inextricably tied to you.

My vision clears even as I gaze at you through its multi-coloured flames of beckoning, as like a willing slave I make myself move even closer to you – pulled by some unseen, pesky force that I cannot be mad at. A room illuminated by beauty so spellbinding that I scarcely blink in fear of losing sight of it even for a fraction of a millisecond.

The flickers are in desperation as they fight to stay alight and not be overshadowed by what nature has over its artificial –your real - the light of you, that is brighter than any light it could shine, even if joined by a million other scented candle lights.

Enraptured by your pheromones, the candle 's scent takes second place; pushed way back in the distance as olfactory's power takes over and thoughts scatter into many different directions at the same time, taking me with them on a ride so wild, I forget for just a breath, where I am and instead, occupy that sphere where I want to be. That place where I am engulfed by you; where scented candles battle with each other to capture your essence and enslave unsuspecting souls.

Love Speaks

Feelings so absolutely potent they move you; to tears, to action, to spaces where words are so unnecessary, as love speaks eloquently; fluent in its own need to express its innermost longings. Expressions more fluent than those deep words spoken by an excited lover, than a preacher at the top of his game, than a poet who so skillfully captures her audience and the lyrics of a song; belted out at its highest octave by he who serenades her.

Uttering those silent words that course through my every being and scream at the top of their lungs that no matter what I am doing, where I am going, who I am with; I have no choice but to hear them. Vocalizations so compelling that I can scarcely escape them; regardless of my temporary reluctance to believe them; running from the intense fear of what they mean for my now and for a future I am afraid to explore; in the present I now occupy.

Love Speaks, and when it does, I am helpless against the power it holds over me, as it wraps itself around that organ that thumps and beats, and I have no resistance left as I am imprisoned by its unmistakable timbre when it reverberates around my very soul; and I become its helpless slave. I listen, I hear & my entire being stands at attention when love speaks....